D060506I

River
Food Chains

Angela Royston

Heinemann
LIBRARY

Chicago, Illinois

Edited by Claire Throp, Diyan Leake and Helen
Cox Cannons
Designed by Joanna Malivoire and Philippa
Jenkins
Original illustrations © Capstone Global
Library Ltd 2014
Picture research by Elizabeth Alexander and
Tracy Cummins
Production by Victoria Fitzgerald
Originated by Capstone Global Library Ltd
Printed in the United States of America in
North Mankato, Minnesota

092014
008486RP

**Library of Congress Cataloging-in-
Publication Data**
Royston, Angela, 1945- author.
  River food chains / Angela Royston.
     pages cm.—(Food chains and webs)
  Includes bibliographical references and index.
  ISBN 978-1-4846-0520-2 (hb)—ISBN 978-1-
4846-0527-1 (pb) 1. Stream ecology—Juvenile
literature. 2. Rivers—Juvenile literature. 3. Food
chains (Ecology)—Juvenile literature. 4. Stream
conservation—Juvenile literature. I. Title.

  QH541.5.S7
  577.6'4—dc23   2013040536

Acknowledgments
We would like to thank the following for
permission to reproduce photographs:
Alamy pp. 12 (© Datacraft – Sozaijiten), 13,
23e, 25 algae (© Trevor Pearson), 16 (© John
Warburton-Lee Photography), 20 (© Juniors
Bildarchiv GmbH), 23b (© Neil McNicoll),
23d (© WildPictures), 25 salmon (© Alaska
Stock), 27 (© Wildscape), 29 (© blickwinkel);
Corbis pp. 21 (© Wim van Egmond/Visuals
Unlimited), 25 otter (© Joe McDonald), 25 trout
(© Ken Lucas/ Visuals Unlimited Inc), 28 (©
Philippe Henry/First Light); Getty Images pp. 19
(DeAgostini), 22 (Flickr RF), 25 crayfish (Steve
Maslowski); Shutterstock pp. 1 (© Igor Kolos),
4 (© zebra0209), 5 (© Greg Amptman), 7 (©
bumihills), 8 (© karamysh), 9 (© Nancy Bauer),
10 (© Christopher Elwell), 11a (© Jan Gottwald),
11b (© Pinosub), 11c (© knin), 11d, 24, 25 fly
larva, 25 snail (© scubaluna), 14 (© anotherlook),
15 (© EBFoto), 17a (© Patrick K. Campbell),
17b (© defpicture), 17c (© Santi Rodriguez), 18
(© Johan Swanepoel/Sergey Uryadnikov), 23a
(© S Kolesnikov), 23c (© EcoPrint), 25 eagle
(© Serjio74), 26 (© Erni); SuperStock p. 17d (©
Stock Connection).

Cover photograph of an eagle fish reproduced
with permission of Shutterstock (wildpix).

We would like to thank Michael Bright for his
invaluable help in the preparation of this book.

Every effort has been made to contact copyright
holders of material reproduced in this book.
Any omissions will be rectified in subsequent
printings if notice is given to the publisher.

All the Internet addresses (URLs) given in this
book were valid at the time of going to press.
However, due to the dynamic nature of the
Internet, some addresses may have changed,
or sites may have changed or ceased to
exist since publication. While the author and
publisher regret any inconvenience this may
cause readers, no responsibility for any such
changes can be accepted by either the author
or the publisher.

Contents

Living in a River 4

World's Biggest Rivers 6

What Is a Food Chain? 8

A European Food Chain 10

Where Do Food Chains Begin? 12

Animal Consumers 14

An Amazon Food Chain 16

Top Predators 18

Living on the Remains 20

A Limpopo Food Chain 22

Food Webs 24

Broken Chains 26

Protecting Food Chains 28

Glossary 30

Find Out More 31

Index 32

Some words are shown in bold, **like this.**
You can find out what they mean by
looking in the glossary.

Living in a River

Rivers begin in hills or mountains. Streams pour downhill and join together to make a river. The river flows more slowly as it crosses flatter land, until it reaches the sea or a lake.

A river begins as a mountain stream.

A manatee lives in slow-moving rivers.

Many animals and plants live and grow in rivers. This book looks at how they need each other to survive.

World's Biggest Rivers

This map shows the world's longest rivers. Some rivers, such as the Amazon River in South America, have other rivers that flow into them. In addition to these mighty rivers, there are thousands of smaller rivers.

The world's largest rivers are shown as blue lines.

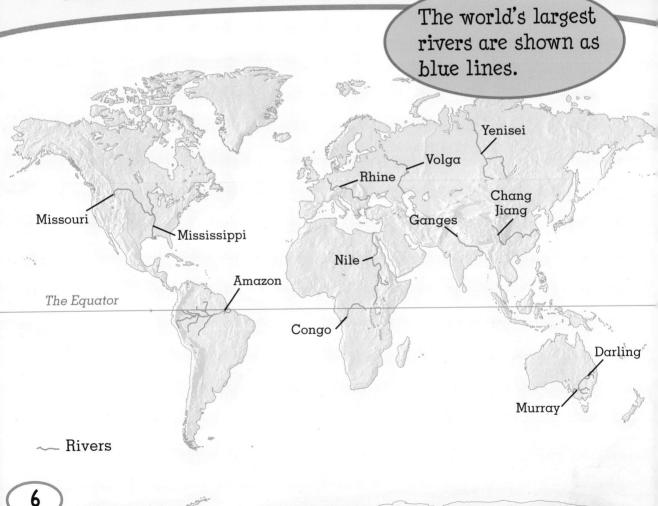

Yenisei

Volga

Rhine

Chang Jiang

Missouri

Ganges

Mississippi

Nile

Amazon

The Equator

Congo

Darling

Murray

～ Rivers

Longest river

The Nile River flows 4,132 miles (6,650 kilometers) from central Africa across the Sahara Desert to the Mediterranean Sea.

What Is a Food Chain?

All living things need food because it gives them **energy**. Without energy, they could not breathe, **digest** food, or swim.

Salmon swimming up a river

Ducks use their bills to get food from the water.

A river **food chain** shows what eats what in the river. The energy in food is passed from plants to each of the animals in the chain.

A European Food Chain

Many different types of living things form a **food chain**. Otters, trout, caddis flies, and pondweed in rivers in Great Britain and Europe form this food chain. **Energy** from the plants passes to the young caddis fly and on to the trout and otter. Without the plants, the whole chain would collapse.

The Severn River flows through part of Great Britain.

Food chain

A trout snatches a young caddis fly

An otter grabs a trout

A young caddis fly feeds on river plants

Pondweed grows in rivers

11

Where Do Food Chains Begin?

The European river **food chain** begins with plants, because plants make their own food. They use sunlight to make sugar, which feeds the whole plant.

Many plants grow in slow-moving rivers.

Too much algae can choke a river with green slime.

Rivers everywhere also contain plants, **algae**, and **plankton**. Plants, algae, and plankton are called **producers** because they make their own food.

Animal Consumers

Animals cannot make their own food. They are called **consumers** because they have to find food in their **habitat** to eat.

A muskrat is an omnivore, but it mostly eats plants.

A heron catches a fish to eat.

Herbivores are animals such as caddis flies and manatees that eat mostly plants. **Carnivores**, such as otters and herons, hunt fish or other animals. Some animals, such as muskrats, eat both plants and animals. They are called **omnivores**.

An Amazon Food Chain

Anacondas, caiman, and piranhas all live in the Amazon River. Piranhas are **omnivores** because they eat seeds and flesh. This **food chain** shows how **energy** passes from the seeds to the piranha, then to the caiman and anaconda.

The Amazon River

Food chain

A huge anaconda can swallow a caiman

A caiman swallows a piranha

Piranhas feed on seeds that have fallen into the water

Seeds float on the river

Top Predators

An anaconda is too big and strong to be hunted by other animals in the Amazon. It is called a top **predator** because it is at the top of its **food chain**. Crocodiles and snapping turtles are top predators in other rivers.

These two crocodiles are on the Nile River.

This snapping turtle eats all kinds of prey, even baby alligators.

Top predators are fierce, but there are always fewer of them than their **prey**. If predators ate up all their prey, they would have nothing left to eat and would soon starve!

Living on the Remains

Piranha fish, snapping turtles, and crayfish are **scavengers** as well as **predators**. Scavengers eat the flesh of dead animals.

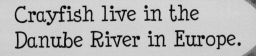

Crayfish live in the Danube River in Europe.

Flatworms are decomposers.

Snails, freshwater crabs, and flatworms are called **decomposers**. They feed on the remains of dead plants and break them up into tiny pieces. Before long, every part of the dead plants and animals is cleared away and recycled.

A Limpopo Food Chain

The Limpopo River flows across southern Africa. In this **food chain, energy** passes from **algae** through the caddis fly to the bullfrog, the yellowfish, and up to the fish eagle. Animals in a food chain are more likely to be eaten when they are young and not fully formed.

The Limpopo River

Food chain

A fish eagle grabs a small yellowfish

A yellowfish snatches a young African bullfrog

A bullfrog feeds on caddis flies

Young caddis flies feed on algae

Algae makes its own food in the river

Food Webs

A **food chain** shows one way in which various plants and animals in a **habitat** are linked. However, most animals eat more than one type of food. A **food web** shows how several animals in a habitat are connected. A food web in North America is shown here on page 25.

Freshwater snails feed on **algae**. The food web on page 25 shows what feeds on the snails.

Food web

American river otter

bald eagle

trout

salmon

caddis fly larva

freshwater snail

American crayfish

algae

Broken Chains

When American crayfish were brought into some British rivers, they almost wiped out the local crayfish. This was because American crayfish carry a disease that kills British crayfish.

An American crayfish crawls out of a British river.

A European crayfish

American crayfish are bigger and fiercer than their European cousins. They damage **food chains** by gobbling up so many water plants, small fish, and snails that there is little food left for other animals.

Protecting Food Chains

People damage **food chains.** Chemicals from farmland and factories pollute the water. Cutting down trees on the riverbanks destroys the **habitat** for beavers and other river animals.

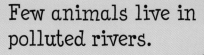

Few animals live in polluted rivers.

People try to protect rivers. For example, beavers have been brought back to some rivers. The beavers' dams create pools, where plants and small animals become food for otters, heron, and fish.

Glossary

algae tiny living things in, for example, green slime. Algae can make their own food.

carnivore animal that eats only the meat of other animals

consumer living thing, particularly an animal, that feeds on other living things, such as plants and other animals

decomposer living thing, such as an earthworm, fungus, or bacterium, that breaks up the remains of plants and animals and turns them into soil

digest break up food into tiny pieces inside the body

energy power needed to do something, such as move, breathe, or swallow

food chain diagram that shows how energy passes from plants to different animals

food web diagram that shows how different plants and animals in a habitat are linked by what they eat

habitat place where something lives

herbivore animal that eats only plants

omnivore animal that eats plants and animals

plankton tiny plants and animals that float near the surface of water

predator animal that hunts other animals for food

prey animal hunted for food

producer living thing, such as a plant, that makes its own food

scavenger animal that feeds off the flesh and remains of dead animals

Find Out More

Books

Facthound offers a safe, fun way to find web sites related to this book. All the sites on Facthound have been researched by our staff.

Here's all you do:

Visit www.facthound.com

Type in this code: 9781484605202

Web sites

education.nationalgeographic.com/education/encyclopedia/
river/?ar_a=1
Find out all about rivers at this National Geographic web site.

wwf.panda.org/about_our_earth/teacher_resources/webfieldtrips/
food_chains/
This WWF web site looks at food chains and food webs.

www.rivers.gov/kids/
This web site gives lots of fun facts for kids about rivers in the United States.

Index

algae 13, 22, 23, 24, 25, 30

Amazon River 6, 16-17

anacondas 16, 17, 18

bald eagles 25

beavers 28, 29

broken food chains 26-27

bullfrogs 22, 23

caddis flies 10, 11, 15, 22, 23, 25

caimans 16, 17

carnivores 15, 30

consumers 14-15, 30

crabs 21

crayfish 20, 25, 26-27

crocodiles 18

decomposers 21, 30

ducks 9

energy 8, 9, 10, 16, 22, 30

fish 8, 16, 17, 20, 22, 23, 25

fish eagles 22, 23

flatworms 21

food chains 9-13, 16-17, 18, 22-23, 24, 27, 30

food webs 24-25, 30

herbivores 14, 15, 30

herons 15, 29

Limpopo River 22-23

longest rivers 6-7

manatees 5, 15

muskrats 14, 15

Nile River 6, 7, 18

omnivores 15, 16, 30

otters 10, 11, 15, 25, 29

piranhas 16, 17, 20

plankton 13, 30

plants 9, 10, 11, 12-13, 15

pollution 28

pondweed 10, 11

predators 18-19, 20, 30

producers 13, 30

protecting food chains 29

salmon 8, 25

scavengers 20, 30

Severn River 10

snails 21, 24, 25, 27

snapping turtles 18, 19, 20

streams 4

sunlight 12

threats to food chains 28

top predators 18-19

trout 10, 11, 25

yellowfish 22, 23